WHOSE HEAVEN IS IT ANYWAY?

Ian F. DeVaney

Illustrations
Shannon O'Sullivan

Whose Heaven Is It Anyway?

©1991 Ian F. DeVaney

ISBN: 0692425705
ISBN-13: 978-0692425701

Printed in USA
by CreateSpace
an Amazon Company

Published by
Ian F. DeVaney
Las Vegas, Nevada 89101

Whose Heaven Is It Anyway?

Table of Contents

The Spirit/Soul Syndrome

Let's suppose – just suppose mind you – that a Human Being and a Spirit or Soul are created, simultaneously, at the moment of conception.

Now if you're getting upset with me don't read any further.

Let's suppose the Baby develops in the womb and is delivered into the world with its personal Spirit intact.

The Spirit isn't any older or smarter than the Baby. They start off even.

The Baby's job is to nourish itself, grow, learn, and put as much time on earth as it can.

The Spirit's job is "Cryptographer." The Spirit classifies, categorizes and files in order of importance all of the activities our body has participated in during this time on earth.

The importance of these job descriptions will become more obvious as we continue our journey towards Heaven, so remember them.

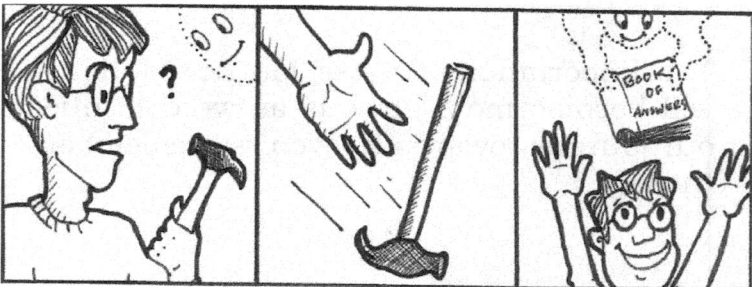

The Spirit as Guide and Guardian

The Spirit is our Subconscious and our Conscience, that inner-self that scolds the Human for being mean or petty. It punishes by keeping the Human from a good night's sleep, at least.

Often, when we cannot recall a name or an incident, we ignore it, and all of a sudden it comes to us. WE GIVE THE CREDIT TO OUR SUBSCONSCIOUS.

Maybe what happened was that we relaxed our conscious mind long enough for our Spirit to get in with the information it had all along but had to wait until it could get a thought in edge-wise.

What a jerk our Spirit must think we are when we keep making the same mistakes over and over when the information we need to prevent it is on call.

We're so busy thinking we know what we're doing that we don't put our mind in neutral long enough to let our Spirit remind us what happened the last time we did that.

When our Conscious is occupied with intense emotions our Spirit can't get through to keep us from doing or saying something stupid.

Getting mad, being frightened, rejoicing, falling in love, lusting...

These are the things that block out our common sense, our Spirit.

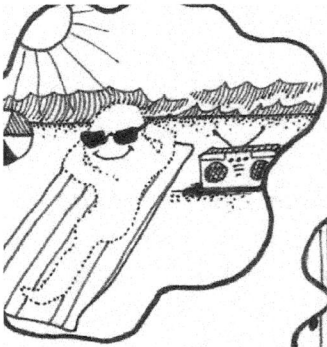

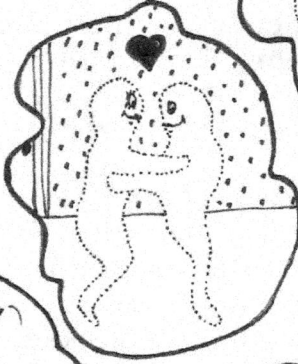

Getting Ready for Heaven

Why, you might ask, is the Spirit going to all of this trouble?

I'll tell you what I think if you promise not to get mad.

This Spirit/Soul is preparing to go to Heaven when the Human Being gives up the Body. The Spirit is going to take all of the good memories, the love, the laughter, the hug of a small child, the feel of a warm sun, the taste of a favorite food, the smell of a baby fresh out of the bath.

With these our Spirit creates its personal Heaven. Our Spirit is leaving the inconvenient task of disposing of the human remains along with all of the painful memories left behind. It leaves the dirty work to someone else. Why should our Spirit feel bad about that? The Spirit's job was record keeping. That mess was the Human's doing. You get rid of it. Besides, that's the way it's been done since the beginning of time.

When Loved Ones Die We Cry

We don't cry because they died. We cry because we'll miss them. We have no concept of death. We don't know what happened to them, where their Spirits went, what their Spirits might be doing, we do know that we can't go with them. We're crying because we're selfish.

Spirits are selfish too. That's why they take everybody they like with them, dead and alive, and do whatever they want, whenever they want to do it, with anyone they want to do it with.
SO THERE!

They died and they took you with them and left you behind in the same instant.

They aren't going to miss you because they will visit with you anytime they want to and you have no choice because WHOSE HEAVEN IS IT ANYWAY?

My Mother has died, my Father has died, and I know where they are. I know who they're with and I know what they're doing.

They are wherever they enjoy being. They are with whoever they enjoy being with. They do whatever they enjoy, with or without me, with or without each other.

Can They Get Away With That?

You bet they can because: It's their Heaven isn't it?

I can leave the cemetery with a lighter heart. If there is a tear in my eye it's because I'm being selfish. I'm still human.

I'm not looking forward to death but I'm not afraid of the Reaper either. The Reaper gets the Human part of me but I know where the real me will be.

I'll be anywhere I want to be and I'll be doing whatever makes me happy!

My Ego makes me believe there will be people crying because I left them behind. My common sense wants to ask them why.

They're not doing anything they want anytime they want to do it, are they?

I should be crying for them, but I'll probably be too busy having fun.

AMEN

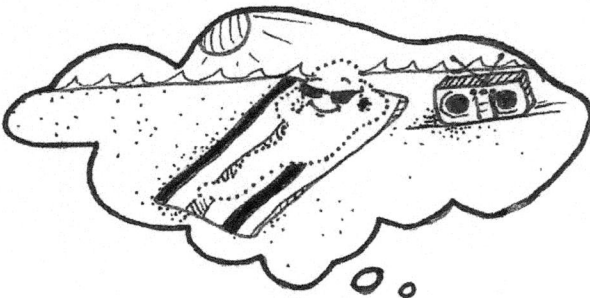

Heaven

Just for the sake of discussion when was the last time you heard a description of HEAVEN that made sense?

It's a little far-fetched to imagine the trillions of people who have died since Adam and Eve gathered together in one place and calling it HEAVEN.

Egad! That's much too far-fetched.

Do we sort them by "Goodness?"

Do we sort them by the kinds of activities they enjoy: Golf, Pool, Cards, Swimming?

OR do we sort them by Religion, Sex, Occupation, Education?

What language will be spoken?

Are we really expecting the PhD's to associate with the D.U.M.B.'S?

I'm not trying to start anything; I don't want people to get mad at me, but I have a theory that you might like to explore with me.

? ? ? ? ? ? ? ? ?

Customized Heaven

We customize our homes, clothes, cars and shoes. We even customize our vacations. What I am suggesting is that you are customizing your own Heaven right now.

TRY THIS:
FIRST: Ask yourself, "What's Heaven really like?" If you come up with an answer, you are way ahead of most of us.
SECOND: Ask anyone "What's Heaven really like?"
THIRD: Be prepared to ask the question again because they're not going to believe they heard you right the first time.
THEN: Brace yourself for anything from a feeble attempt at an answer, to an outright insult.

I'm not so egotistical as to think I am the first one to come up with this idea. I suspect the rest of my ilk are locked up somewhere for their own protection.

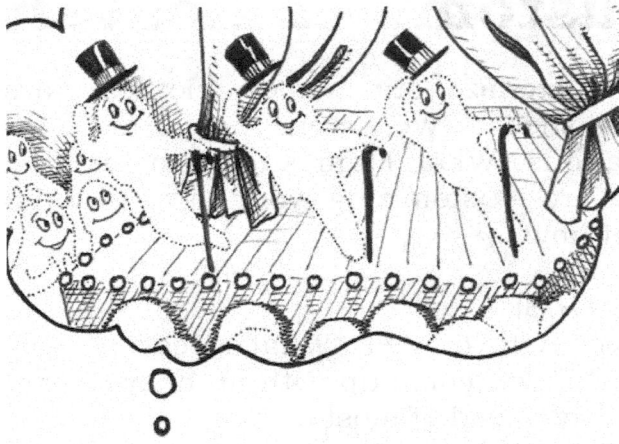

Dreams

What is a Dream? Why do we Dream? If you're still humoring me listen to this.

A Dream is our Spirit entertaining itself. The Spirit doesn't need nourishment and it doesn't need sleep. So, while the Human is recuperating from its daily activities, and the Spirit has finished recording the memories of the day, why not have some fun? Let's rehash some of the good times we've already had. Let's Dream!!!

Dreams could be thought of as a preview of Heaven we're planning. Nightmares could be Heavenly Rejects! Ugh! There's some stuff we don't want to take along. Yeah, yeah, I know what you're thinking. "That's pretty asinine Logic."

I don't know what you think about out-of-body experiences but I think it's the Spirit getting a head start on the fact of death. Here is this Spirit thinking it's all over and heading for the heaven it's been dreaming about, and its Human counterpart decides not to go. Now the Spirit has to come back.

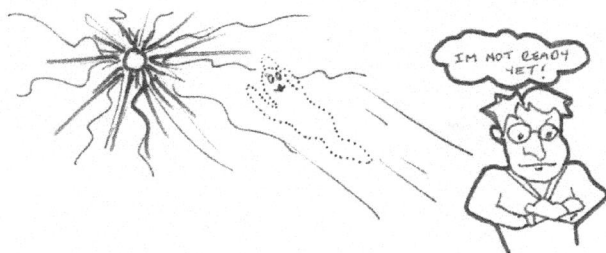

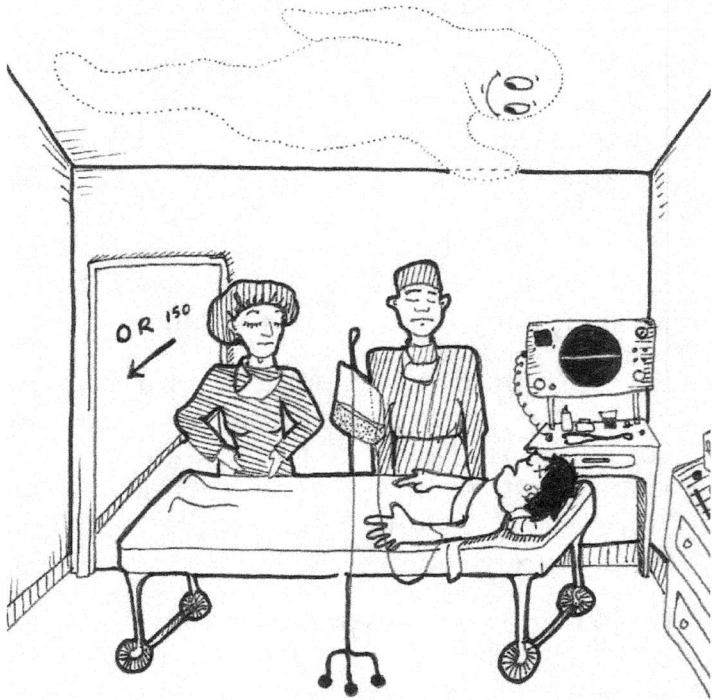

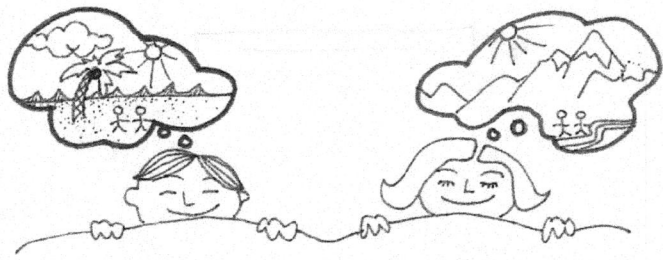

Dreams 2

How else do you explain the stories of entering a brightly lit place filled with deceased loved ones, a wonderful feeling of contentment and then winding up back in this bag of bones we call a Human Being?

And, try to explain stories of a person having watched from above while doctors operate on them. Was their Spirit jumping the gun?

Let's take a look at Dreams and Dreaming.

Two people are in the same bed; both are dreaming. One of them is dreaming that both of them are on the beach in Hawaii. The other one is dreaming they are both on a picnic in the Colorado Mountains.

These Dreamers aren't in each other's way.

These Dreams aren't colliding with each other.

These people took the person they wanted to be with to a place they wanted to be, doing what they wanted to do. The other person had no choice and didn't care, because they were with the person they wanted to be with, doing what they wanted to do.

Could this be Heaven?

More Dreams

A career military man dreams of a battle, people around him dying. These people don't care if they are dying in his Dream because they are really in a Dream of their own design having a great time. Are you going to tell him to "Knock it off?"

A Cat Burglar Dreams of climbing up a skyscraper, prying open a window, creeping around a dark room with a flashlight and scooping up somebody's valuables.

Hey, "Whose Heaven Is It Anyway?"

Remember that dog you loved so much? The one everybody else hated? HE'LL BE THERE.

Remember that individual you had to kiss up to that turned your stomach? NOT THERE.

"IF YOU'RE NOT NICE TO ME WHILE I'M HERE. I WON'T TAKE YOU WITH ME WHEN I GO."

Think about that the next time you're tempted to say something nasty to someone you love.

Ghosts

No one will argue that there are some not-too-bright Human Beings.

Maybe a Ghost is a not-too-bright Spirit.

Let's be kind and assume there were some mitigating circumstances. Perhaps the Spirit was immature.

If a Spirit refuses to leave, where would it go?

What would it do?

Remember, the Human and the Spirit start out even. The Spirit cannot mature any faster than the Human.

(The Spirit can only record what its Human can comprehend.)

Ipso facto: A deranged Human Being nurtures a deranged Spirit, an Evil Spirit.

In other words, an Evil Spirit has managed to enter and share the Human of another Spirit.

Maybe the Psychiatrist or Hypnotist has managed to eliminate the middle man (the Conscious) and contact the Spirit/Soul directly.

Ghosts 2

A morose Human Being nurtures a sad, wandering Spirit who has refused to enter what it perceives as an Eternity of Anguish and manages to enter another Human Being's body, creating multiple personalities. Who can deny that many Spirits <u>could</u> occupy one Human?

Now we have the Spirit who refuses to leave Earth and refuses to seek refuge in another Human Body.

There poor Souls (Spirits) are the Ghosts of our Past, Present, and Future. They wander, they haunt, they cry, they search for that elusive emotion called Happiness.

These poor Souls wouldn't recognize Happiness if it landed in their lap, so they wander through Eternity, moaning, wailing, and weeping.

Even God can't help these poor devils.

I HAVE JUST DESCRIBED HELL.

Is this explanation of heaven any more difficult to accept that any other?
Does it parallel what religions teach?
Be a good person and go to heaven
Heaven is a pleasant and peaceful place.
No bad things happen in heaven.

My theory explains how Heaven is possible for everyone, regardless of religious beliefs, or the lack of them.

Hypnotism

An abnormal mental state resembling sleep.

What really happens during a Hypo-session? Does the Hypnotist put the conscious mind asleep in order to have an uninterrupted chat with our "Cryptographer?"

Don't ask the mechanic about your eyes and don't ask the Optometrist about your carburetor.

The conscious mind is littered with opinions. The Spirit has the facts, no need to stumble around remembering, it knows.

The Hypnotist can ask our Spirit to relive past experiences, not remember them.

If the Hypnotist asks the Spirit not to tell the conscious mind what it revealed to the Hypnotist it doesn't.

We awaken from our "Abnormal" sleep remembering nothing that has just taken place.

If there is more than one Spirit why wouldn't that Spirit reveal itself/themselves?

Psychoanalysis: Process of studying the unconscious mind.

OR

Hypnotism: Process of studying the Spirit within.

Epilogue

The serious side of me wants to believe what I have supposed within these covers. How much easier it would be to accept death, both for our loved ones and ourselves, if we could believe in this explanation of passing over.

If anyone has given a blueprint of the journey from here to there I missed it.

Everything I have heard sounds like "Jump, I'll catch you."

The notion of Heaven is "Blind Faith."

Having traveled around the world, walked and talked with the working class and played with their children, I cannot conceive of a lesser Heaven for these non-believers.

The working class around the world want the same thing. They want to feed, clothe and house their family.

The working class around the world <u>don't</u> want the same thing. They <u>don't</u> want to shoot, bomb or inflict injury on anyone and they <u>don't</u> want anyone to shoot, bomb or inflict injury on them.

If war were put to a vote, guess what?

Nobody has experienced Heaven first hand.

If Heaven were put to a vote could we expect the same result?

Author
Ian F. DeVaney

Born 1935 in Lansing, Michigan. Not my idea or my fault.

I lock myself out of my car, trip over curbs, get in the left turn lane at the wrong intersection, get drunk at the wrong times and still think I'm pretty smart.

I'm the dummy with the half gallon of ice cream in the wrong lane at the super market.

All in all I'm a lot like you.

I like having my own way. I don't always get it but I always like having it.

At the age of 50 I pre-arranged my own funeral and paid for it. Even after I'm gone I'll be having my own way.

I'm in excellent health and have a "Living Will" with Durable Power of Attorney for Health Care Decisions so that I will not be kept alive longer that would be prudent.

There has never been a period in my life I did not have to work for a living.

I have worked in a factory.

I have driven a taxicab.

I have been a delivery man.

I have been in business for myself.

I have worked for a large corporation.

I have worked my way around the world as a merchant seaman.

I feel I am entitled to an opinion.

I worked for it!!!

Contact information: devaneyif@juno.com

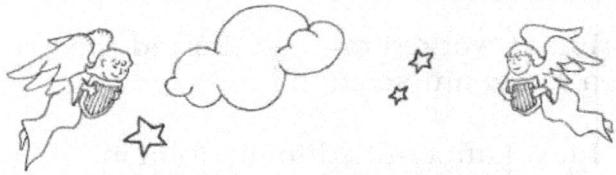

Acknowledgement

My appreciation to Shannon O'Sullivan for providing the wonderful illustrations for **Whose Heaven Is It Anyway?**

www.ingramcontent.com/pod-product-compliance
Lightning Source LLC
Chambersburg PA
CBHW060552030426
42337CB00019B/3518